The Earthen Flute
collected and new verses

Kiriti Sengupta

Illustrations
Tamojit Bhattacharya

Hawakal Publishers

Published by **Hawakal Publishers**
185, Kali Temple Road, Nimta, Calcutta 700049, India.

First edition: February, 2016
Revised second edition: October, 2016
Third edition, India (Hardbound): September, 2018
Third edition (Paperback): September, 2018

Printed and bound: S. P. Communications, Raja Dinendra
Chandra Street, Calcutta 700009.

Contact: Bitan Chakraborty (Founder, Hawakal)
Email: info@hawakal.com

© 2018 Kiriti Sengupta

All rights reserved. No part of this publication may be
reproduced or transmitted (other than for purposes of review/
critique) in any form or by any means, electronic or mechanical,
including photocopy, recording, or any information storage
and retrieval system without prior permission in writing from
the publisher or the copyright holder where applicable. The
author asserts his moral right to be identified as the author of
his work.

Cover concept, painting and design: Tamojit Bhattacharya

ISBN-13: 978-93-87883-27-7 (Hardbound)
ISBN-13: 978-93-87883-07-9 (Paperback)
Price: INR Three hundred only (Rs. 300/- only)

"...I see the Past, Present and Future, existing all at once
Before me; O Divine Spirit, sustain me on thy wings!
That I may awake Albion from his long and cold repose..."

The Earthen Flute is dedicated to the "glorious luminary,"
William Blake.

Acknowledgements

I'm grateful to the editors of *Dukool, Grey Sparrow Journal, Wilderness House Literary Review,* and *Dead Snakes* blog for publishing a few poems that have been included in this collection.

I'm thankful to my publisher, Bitan Chakraborty, founder of Hawakal Publishers, for his motivation and zeal.

Heartfelt thanks to Dustin Pickering, who was the first reader and wrote a brilliant foreword.

Love and blessings to Prabir Roy, Shouvanik Dey Banerjee and Tanmoy Bhattacharjee for being my strength.

Sincere gratitude to my reviewers and critics.

Did I mention my family? I will cease to exist without their support in all possible forms. Love you, Ma, Baba, Bhaswati and Aishikk.

And finally, I belong to you, my readers!

Dare a Poet Apologize?

In this small volume of delightful verses, Kiriti Sengupta speaks again of the human condition and the hidden truth of religion. The two remain inseparable in his work altogether. An odd affirmation of life is shaped here in this volume: Sengupta, in an age when so much is taken for granted and our strongest blessings are seen as hindrances, directs us to the somethings we have missed. As the poetic work draws toward its end he makes an interesting comparison, whether intentionally or by chance. He reflects on his engagement ring after comparing civilization to a diamond. The symbolism here implies we are married metaphorically to our condition, and the fact that he ties his engagement ring with the sense of "what is missing" reveals his feeling for the skeptical pessimism driving the contemporary world. He believes it is humanity in its nonage, still kicking in the womb.

In "Mother Water," our earth is further recognized as a womb and Sengupta clarifies that this womb, like a mother's womb, is built to withstand force, penetration, stretching, and suffering. The Ganga absorbs the fallen and the dead into its mouth. It swells; it fills the persons of Hinduism with reverence and awe. It is recognized that this swelling river is a force itself, and not just an expression of force. It swallows the dead, cleanses the earth, and by its violent motions is a concentrated power that demands adulation. Its furies are the callings of the dead to the living to live and heal.

The poem "Kajal Deeghi" also employs intense water symbolism.

"Leisure around the water
It was named Kajal Deeghi"

In this poem, a woman's eyes are compared to a lake and the poet is enticed into them. They appear to be a "bird's nest" that is both a home, and reflection. This implicates that thought resides within, and the eyes are thought's deepest expression outwardly.

There is also the poem the title is taken from, "Cryptic Idioms." This is an interesting poem because it asks an age-old question. The answer is revealed in these lines: *"A flute sounds along the serpentine track/ Breath tunes it from mute to high … to crack!"* This is a powerful discussion invoked. In political and scientific terms, the poet defines catastrophe theory, laws of emergence, and social complexity. He performs this feat in two simple lines. I am a poet obsessed with political theory and how natural science explains many things beside the material world. All natural things (all existing and living things are part of the natural world in some way, even literature) abide by the laws of nature. There is analysis of the dispersion of fairy tales across cultures using the same methods developed in genetics. A collection of poems, without the knowledge of the poet, follows a rhythm and develops its own rules according to inherent laws of nature that science seeks to uncover. Troy Camplin, interdisciplinary scholar, discusses the "fractal distribution" of words in Thomas Hardy's *Jude the Obscure*. In this amazing essay, he finds patterns of word repetitions and analyzes their essential fractal geometry. This essay, "Introduction to the Fractal Distribution of Words in a Text," is available online at www.academia.net.

This collection is not nearly as simple as it appears. Let's take a look at "Let The Flowers Bloom". The prose poem is highly symbolic of Indian history. This piece is a small miracle of literature. Ultimately, the young boy recalls an India of the Copper Age. The Continent hasn't been the same after Partition. Bangladesh and

India, once of the same continent, are currently shaped by relations of either-or. Sometimes accepting each other as neighbors and at other moments falling into disputes over immigration, the Ganges River waters that Bangladeshis feel robbed of, border disputes, the shortsighted statement of political leaders, or several other things that stir tension, Bangladesh and India are still part of the same soul. The symbolic use of the familiar "Uncle" expresses a sense of discontinuity — who is India really? Partition and religious conflict wrecked the continent, confusing identity. Sengupta assesses the problem fairly in other parts of the collection, as in "Do You Have a Christian Name?":

> *"But now I have altered my answer*
> *I say:*
> *'I'm not sure if Jesus offered names…'"*

The most intriguing part of this poem is how subtle the historical question is posed: "*A name is usually pre or post-natal?*" Sengupta firmly negates this assumption of his own in the poem.

Listen to this wordsmith with his delicate use of depth metaphor, calmness and brevity in language, and subtlety of speech. He truly has a vision, and it is a writer's vision of the world. It defies political realities and ideologies, and it asserts the truly human spirit. The human heart is spoken of bravely, in its lusts and wars, its struggles and despair, its intention to overcome. Hope isn't toyed with in these poems because the author is brazenly serious, and he does not intend to fool you. But, like a poet, he stuns you with wordplay, imagination, and webs of wisdom. Listen: we know the world suffers. There is nothing we can do. The poet can promise the end of war, a reunion of brothers and sisters, the unity of a war torn country, the happiness of a widow. Art, the hope of our hidden world of complexity, is a light, a shadow cast by alternating and residual struggle: art, it is the lion, the breakfast we savor, the eagle come to sky … art, the reminder we are human; and no matter how old, we are still children seeking refuge in hope, a tearful night in our Mother's lap with her breast to our mouths.

Kiriti Sengupta says what is said in these poems. However, much more is spoken in the crevices of his thought and the steering of his river of wisdom.

There is nothing seeking apology here.

Dustin Pickering
January 24, 2016
[Editor-in-Chief of *Harbinger Asylum* and
Founder of Transcendent Zero Press, Houston, Texas]

"You wrote on Padmavati; you fetched Radha in your poetry," a reader inquisitively asked if I had considered the Western population. I got another inquirer who was even smarter, "Aren't you promoting a superstition in the form of a tabeez?" It was my pleasure to address their queries. I told the former, "If you read poetry you must learn to appreciate symbols." The latter heard it right as I said, "You call it superstition, but I would rather name it civilization."
Poetry is an occasion for rejoicing ... celebrating the earth, birth and exit through the earthen flute. After all, poets are not beggars, but seekers of the truth!

Kiriti Sengupta
January 25, 2016
Calcutta, India

APPRECIATIONS

Sengupta has an uncanny way of mixing memory and myth. The earthly and the ethereal coalesce in these meditative poems to create a rare poetic experience.

— *K Satchidanandan*

"Prayers carry lives within" as do these luminous and varied poems: some, brief as a firefly's single pulse from the darkness, some, brightly lit as the long bridge between cultures. These poems dwell a language beyond the many borders of languages. You owe it to yourself to read these poems right now, not so much as to get out of your *"self"* as to come inside.

— *Lorna Dee Cervantes*
(Olympia, Washington)

The Earthen Flute is an elegiac song daring us to reexamine our relationship — or lack thereof — with the natural world. "Womb" addresses our pedestrian tendency to shift our focus on Mother Nature only after a natural disaster has occurred when the speaker utters, *"With every earthquake I realize/ I have failed to express/ Much attention/ To my mother."* The messages

vii

throughout, though, are not all warnings; they're calls to action for us to not overlook the beauty in the ordinary and witness "[how] *a wonderful world opens up deep inside*" whether it's observing a Bengali widow inserting bread in a toaster or feeling empathy when "*A father's heart succumbs/ As his daughter awaits the groom.*" Few poets can harness emotion with spirituality and offer crucial insight; after reading "Let The Flowers Bloom," you'll agree that Sengupta is one of them.

— *Jonathan Moody*
author of *Olympic Butter Gold*

Sengupta's poems range from the spiritual to the prosaic, from soaring perspective to minute detail, and they constantly remind us that the world in which we live, the earth, the water, the sky and the enduring pattern of life, is much bigger than our small concerns.

— *Casey Dorman*
Editor, *Lost Coast Review*

Sengupta's poems occasionally dwell on the seamy side of our existence, and thus, impel readers to identify the agony hidden under the veiled rapture of human life. *The Earthen Flute* sets the tune of religiosity in a different perspective and tries to analyze the strange connection between religion and humanity through poetic imagery.

— *World Literature Today*

The Earthen Flute has a language so delicate that it crumbles at every ostensible reading. The delightful part is that the poet is clearly aware of that — Sengupta knows he belongs to an era where one cannot denote silence by simply writing "silence" and they need four blank pages to denote that profundity. [The collection] is like a Constable or a Turner painting of a beautiful edifice on a sunny day — splashes of watercolor and the subtle details, which are delightfully delicate.

—*The Statesman*

[Sengupta] is not a cerebral poet; he is the poet of ether, water, earth and the senses. [*The Earthen Flute*] interrogates the premise of language. Some poems are written in snatches, some employ narratives, some take off into the world of the ordinary, and some are of spiritual intensity embodied by river, God or purely otherworldly concerns. Some look at the dialectics of old age and youth, while some look at temporality — of death or even of material living. [Sengupta] points to a world beyond the worldly, not affecting voices of religiosity or re-birth, but a world where life has been fulfilled — the life of love, carnal desires, veneration for Him, life of the poor or the rustic, also a life of incandescent Nature. That is why one would call him a Romantic poet in the tradition of the great Romantics where idealism, pantheism and humanism work in poetic order. There is a tradition to fall back in Kiriti Sengupta's poetry. It is the tradition of the chant, the song or the *geet*. One is reminded of the chants of Mira*bai* or Kabir, this eclectic strain runs through his poems almost beatifically. [*The Earthen Flute*] is remarkable poetry and a gutsy breakaway from contemporary poetry, written in the English language, in India today.

— *The Lake*

[These] poems thrive in portraying emotions that in some quaint way expose the hidden beauty of the world and throw a new light on life's most common trivialities. Sengupta surveys the world about him not as a callow idealist, or as an imaginative dreamer, but as the exponent of the ethic of acceptance. Actually in *The Earthen Flute* [he] is concerned with the pageant of life. The distinctive feature of his diction is density of meaning — many-leveled and metaphorical through and through. [Sengupta] achieves a rare blend of simplicity and depth with an eye for aptness and elegance barely to be found in much of the poetry written today.

— *Red Fez Magazine*

[Sengupta] pipes to his readers very simple (though seemingly problematized), earthly—hence factual—ditties just as Blake would by juxtaposing 'innocence' and 'experience.'

[Sengupta], like Blake, too believes in the reinstatement of contraries of good and evil side by side. [*The Earthen Flute*] gives its readers beauty, reminds them of some faraway music, the smell of the rain drenched earth, first love, the empty eve of *Durga Dashami* (after goddess Durga is immersed in the river), a sexual aftermath, "gathering swallows twitter(ing) in the skies," or, say, a "sunny pleasure dome with caves of ice," but with a postmodernist's expression.

— *Setu Journal*

This collection pulls the reader through Sengupta's daily life as he tunes a fine juxtaposition between the outside world and the emotional side of the inner self. *The Earthen Flute* is a book of poetry for the spiritualist, or for someone looking to connect with their "Essential Nature."

— *The Luxembourg Review*

Kiriti Sengupta's new book of poems dwells on Indian spirituality.

—*Millennium Post*

The Earthen Flute documents human travails and an eternal search for the divine principle for a post-modern audience busy in mass consumption. It is a return successful to our original state of being.

— *Yellow Chair Review*

Table of Contents

Keep An Eye

Among those three eyes of Durga
The third one has been the same
Over the ages

It has been kept open
Full or half

Sculptors never bothered

They have been experimental
Only on her earthly eyes

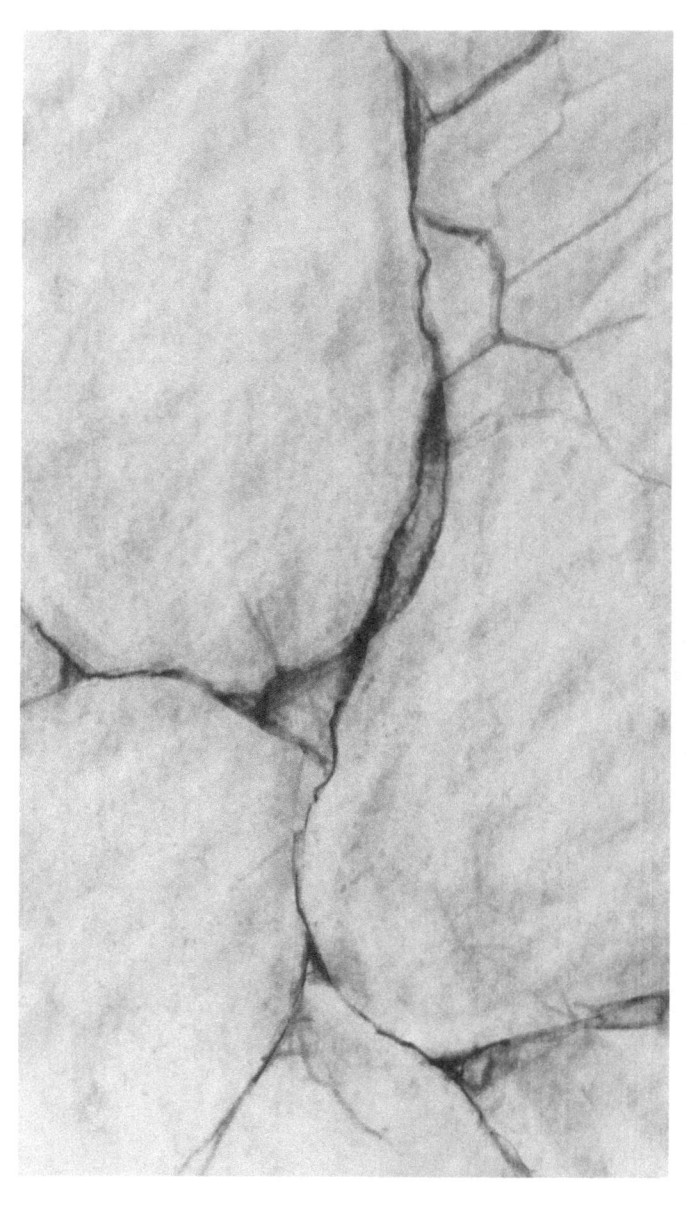

Womb

With every earthquake I realize
I have failed to express
Much attention
To my Mother

She has a right to
Take me into her
Again

I know she will take
Enough care
As she took before

World, you may comment on material loss
Only Mother understands her rupture pain

Moon— The Other Side

Memories unveil themselves
Through snapshots;
The moon has its glory
Pinned in poetry

Elegance, or marks of disgrace,
You may argue,
For not all can be
hunky-dory
With brushes soaked in
Colors of passion
And much hunger

Do you remember the bread
Sukanta left behind?
It was baked in
The blaze of a full moon night

A tombstone may ask for
Flowers, and tears,
While frank hunger can only be fed
By some food to eat

If you can remember,
Moon has its share of crevices
With restricted entry of light
Love
And sheer delight

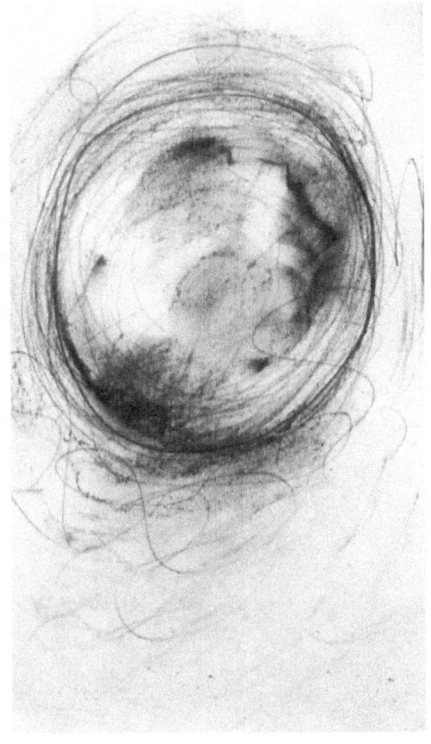

[Note: Sukanta Bhattacharya was a Bengali poet and a key
figure of modern Bengali poetry. His poetry is characterized
by social rebel, patriotism and humanism. In a poem "Hey
Mohajibon" ("Thou, Great Soul") Sukanta wrote: "A world
affected by hunger is too prosaic; the full moon resembles a
toasted bread"]

Kajal Deeghi

Leisure around the water
It was named Kajal Deeghi

I was inquisitive,
Water here didn't look black,
Nor would I call it green.
The lake seemed deep.
I quickly remembered *Banalata Sen.*
Her profound eyes resembled
The nest of a bird.
Those eyes,
Water in the lake
They house, and reflect...

[A *Deeghi* is a lake that is formed naturally. *Kajal* is a widely
used color used by the Asian women for defining their eyes]

Experience Personified

As I walk along an abandoned playground
In the morning, I see new grasses bathed
In the dew of dawn
Putting off my shoes I stand barefooted
and walk again

Tiny droplets envelop my feet
And permeate the skin of my toes

I don't call it a feeling,
I would rather name it
My experience

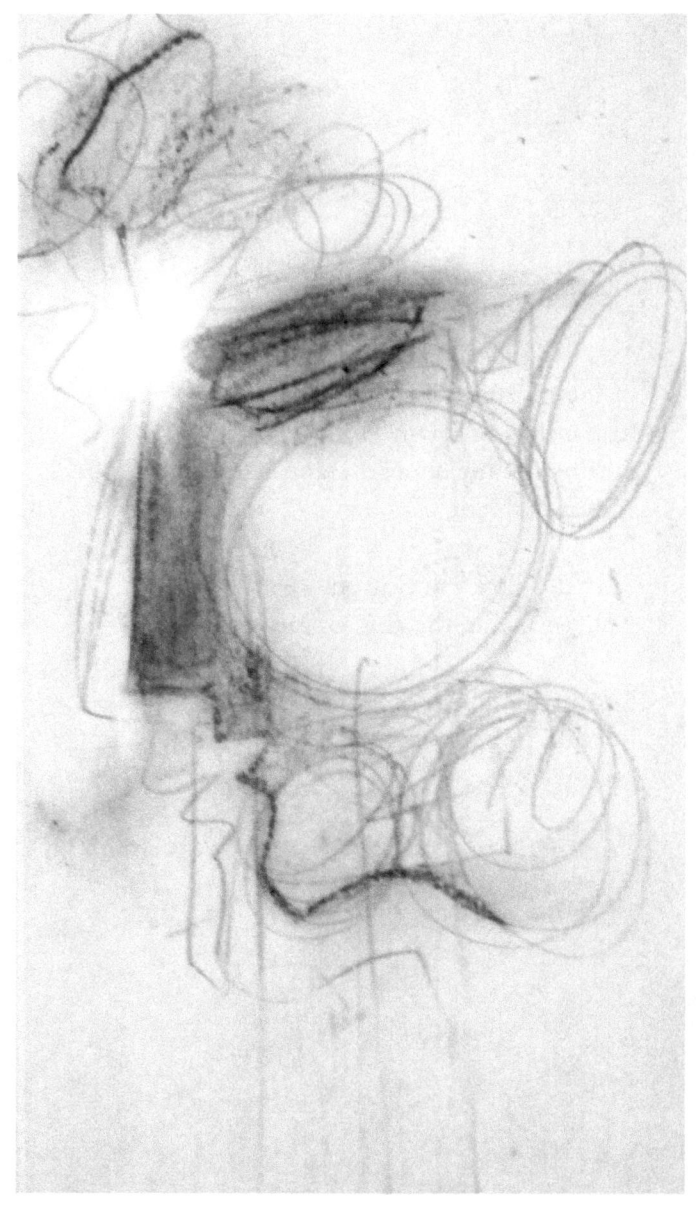

Gateway To God

Prayers carry lives within
They are expressions
Our desires take refuge in—

For all worldly pleasures and fulfillment
We remain scared, perhaps

Wishes are chanted with closed eyes
And we continue to live being frightened

Like an inevitable death
An enormous God steps in

Envy

Jealous—
A Dentist can say if you are one

Your teeth deviate from
The occlusal table
And thus, lips suffer from bites

Do You Have A Christian Name?

People tend to ask me hesitantly
if I have a Christian name
They are aware
I've been baptized long time back

I used to tell them:
"A name is usually pre or post-natal!"

But now I have altered my answer,
I say:
"I'm not sure if Jesus offered names…"

A Different Ballgame

One fine morning you wake up to realize
your poetry
has never been reviewed
You can now plan and think,
if I may suggest:

Redoing all your old stuff;
replacing the words
with synonyms as found on Google,
or in Oxford Advanced Learners, and then
submit them to journals
where editors boast about their high standards
Or
Leave your old stuff as it is,
and think about the classic poets,
the masters,
who were explored
as they set out for their heavenly abode

Petty mind;
it is yet to grasp
houses are made home
only in the earth!

Clean Gene

Rina works as a therapist in a beauty salon. Her office enjoys a nation-wide network, and now they wish to reach out to global customers. Rina meets her clients, she talks to them and listens to the problems they are suffering from. She lends patient hearing, and her skilled suggestions are well received. Rina has a radiating skin that often fetches compliments... During a client meet someone inquired, "Rina, you look so gorgeous. Did you ever have an acne or two?" Rina took no time to answer, "You know, I'm genetically blessed with a clean skin!"

Time And Tide

It was 8 am and the butler inquired, "What would you like to have for your breakfast, Sir?" We partied last night with a group of young ladies. We had good food with plenty of drinks. I cautiously ordered a slice of bread and a cheese omelet. I heard the boy instructing a woman-cook. It was an open kitchen arrangement, and I saw a Bengali widow in her late forties placing the bread-slice in the toaster. She set the time and quickly picked two eggs from the basket. I noticed her eyes as she broke the eggs.

The boy served me breakfast on a white dish. The bread was perfect, but the omelet looked weird. I could make out the woman did not whisk the yolks properly. A bit annoyed with the quality of service, I asked the waiter, "Is she a new appointee?" He hesitantly replied, "She is my aunt, Sir. She lives in our ancestral home. She lost her husband when she was only eighteen!"

Clues To Name

An experiment I undertook. A seed slept in
dark, clueless; no viable chant ... what if
awakened by a mantra? A syllable to prefix and
suffix, and thus was my pride and prejudice!
Got confined, even as I wish to move on. Now
the pride is dear; dearer than my dearest.

Following some cunning way I was keen to
taste some greatness. A tree stands with its green
veil. Through its branches I noticed the ascent
of sap, but it had no salt. Some names sweet
... some seeds added at source!

As one finds it apt! Just the way the mind seeks.
My mind. Mantra bears lust ... petty you, you
blame the luster! Lust reinstated ... inevitable
it is.

Immersion via the mirror ... goodbye to the
goddess, but the lion keeps awake with his eyes
closed. His eyes are terrific ... mesmerizing, or
giving all as I surrender. The first involves
mixing while the latter denotes craving!

Deviations bring popularity ... endless celebrations. Fists full of water and free donation ... serving the pilgrims. Withdrawal reversed.

Complete bath and a full dip ... no excuses, please ... be it the pollution sick! You sprinkle drops, however ... your wisdom runs into the lustrous hole. Incenses are not burnt by wet hands, they say. Prohibited it is. Water has no call, no décor either; it floats the bone and the mortal frames free!

Cryptic Idioms

on Yoga Sutras by Patanjal

1.
I say *Yama* and you think of
The god of death

I said *Yama,*
But I meant the laws of restraint

Meditating on loss in the world of lives
Is but being dispassionate

2.
Disgusting, you wrote, as I asked you to fill in the blank
Too many laws make life—

You could have written: Hell
Isn't it the place where *Yama* dwells?

Balanced blend of more than one liquor
Makes an enjoyable cocktail

3.
You have been practicing
A few postures for health and fun
Kali never fails to show
Her long bloody tongue!

4.
A flute sounds along the serpentine track
Breath tunes it from mute to high … to crack!

For eons religion or its absence
Appears back-to-back

5.
Withdrawal has its share of symptoms
Like a disease—
They both deserve care; they prefer
Nature, countryside over metropolis

6.
Impeccable marketing since the inception of
Communication
Not a gimmick, but *Yoga* at its creative best

Patanjal must be happier now, I bet

Advertisement suggests:
Sir*ji*, "An idea can change your life!"

7.
Much hassles to envision the self—
A mirror fractures to kill the dreams
Neither lenses, nor a pair of glass,
But thick skin that keeps my eye covered
And I patiently await
Unveiling

Trust me, the eye can see

No sorrows anymore, nor a hint of delight
A wonderful world opens up deep inside

Seventh Heaven

Justifications of the earthly
And under-ground affairs sound cliché

Earth is where I wish to live, while
Padmavati prefers her home beneath the ground
One of the hindrances being 'hell'
The mosquitoes, flies and even
                    the butterflies create troubles

Let them be; never mind if they are cheap

Do you consider proverbs demanding?

I won't even try the lane that
                does not lead to your home—
No matter if you say this for several times
My heart beats faster or slower than the normal rate
It won't listen to other lines
It won't say anything either

I'll now walk along the road; what about you?

Hold my hands, and take me along—
Enough of your so-called innocence

Look at the roadside plaque; it says—
Wait for a minute here, o' trespassers
Don't tell me your legs ache
As you climb the stairs to the heaven
Don't you bear love in your soul?

In the name of *Radha*
Your love has condensed
The peacock-tail signs a mark on *Radha*'s forehead

Come on, would you blame the traffic every time
You arrive late?

I'm not a pervert, take a note!
I'm a woman as long as I'm dynamic
I'm a woman unless I'm stilled

Do you think of a woman's voyage to the heaven?

My soul seeks, but the eyes fail to see
They remain closed in the terminal destination
It is a habit, I believe
However, I can now take rest and unwind for a while

Is it morning?

Much excitement prevails
Seems like I'm inside an insulated tube
And my heroine lures and sings

Why won't *Radha* be annoyed?

Nucleus

Self-centeredness is an evil
The sages proclaim!
No 'self' nor the centeredness...

Look,
Barring the 'I'
'Love you' has gone viral

Exploring the implications of the word 'eternal'
Has it anything to do with
Conventional or natural?

What if someone is not straight?

A father's heart succumbs
As his daughter awaits the groom

Tiny pieces of chocolate live in the cookies
And when they surface
I call it 'hide and seek'

There is an old woman with her older man
In the vast of the sky
While the stars smile and twinkle

Interesting indeed!

What would you like me to buy for your Mom?

As you find right, darling!
Don't go overboard;
Do adhere to your budget of
A few hundred rupees

In an acute state of poverty
I hear the sound of husking
Seems like my heaven

The burner never fires,
Nor does the vessel burn

No ash is formed
And a *Kulo* does not fit into the equation

[Note: *Kulo* is a traditional cane-plate commonly used in Bengali
households. As the famous proverb runs: A broken *Kulo* is
employed only to dispense ashes.]

Let The Flowers Bloom

Elderly *Mujibar* has no money; he owns a hovel and a large pond. *Mujibar* eats rice and boiled *Shapla* as he returns from work. He grows *Shapla* in the pond that also has Lotus in it. *Mujibar* picks both the flowers and keeps them in bunches before he vends the flowers in the market. His five-year-old son fails to understand which bunch will be used in their kitchen, and what goes into the Hindu household.

A white Lotus turns red as the Sun rises high in the sky. *Mujibar* has no clue to the occurrence, and considers it a phenomenon. His little son rushes to the veranda and stretches his brown arms in the sunlight.

Leaving behind his little son alone *Mujibar* dies of uncontrolled fever! In the afternoon the small boy wanders around the paddy field, and in the morning he works in the tea-stall adjacent to his hut. He serves tea in small glasses to the customers.

The small boy grows up a bit; people call him by the name *Robi*. On a chilly winter morning a *fakir* arrives at the tea-stall. He does not have warm clothing. *Robi* approaches the *fakir*, "My father has given me a roof, but I have no sky to look at."

The *fakir* offers a tiny copper-box, a *tabeez*, which is considered holy. He suggests, "Chain it around your neck, my son!" *Robi* protests, "Hey, you gave me a piece of copper while I asked for the sky?" The *fakir* urges enthusiastically, "Come on, it is filled with my prayers. I have given you a mountain, rather. You now break through the roof you have."

No magic, but sheer trust enriched with the flavor of innocence! *Robi* does not work anymore; he enjoys a never ending stay in his hut as he cherishes the saintly mountain. The roof remains unchanged; the moon does not arrive. A slice of the sky does not even appear despite *Robi*'s uninterrupted wanting for it. He holds the *tabeez* tightly in his grip, and while looking at the roof he murmurs, "I won't offer you a drape if I don't get a bird."

A bird flutters its wings, and the sound is pretty familiar. Not a crow, nor a heron — some unknown bird. It keeps standing in the mud-pad. A few flowers are visible, and they are not *Shapla*. *Robi* feels warm, his arms, especially the spine region, as if there is a sudden rush of hot water along the spinal duct!

A fragrant ambience sets in while the bird floats up in the air. *Robi's* face attracts drops of mud from the flying bird. Handful of soil, and the hut is flooded with sunlight that enters from the broken roof. *Robi* feels much warmer now. A milkman knocks the door, "Collect milk in the can, *chacha!*"

Notes: *Shapla* (Water Lily) is the national flower of Bangladesh. The flower and its stem are edible. A *tabeez* is a metallic case (square, rectangular, round or oval in shape) that is believed to exert worldly benefits to its users. Lotus is the national flower of India, and it is used in Hindu households in religious rituals. *Chacha* is someone who is considered the brother of one's father.

Mother Water

Ganga has her stories to tell
Wish she had someone to listen to her
Story of her arrival is passé, we guess,
And that of her passage over the ages,
Witnessing numerous banks of civilizations

We are not even bothered to see her struggle
She fights as the boats ply in the river
She accommodates them,
Their loads, and of course men
Physiologists say the womb can withstand
Much stress, and strain

Ganga listens to our prayers
Both mute and loud,
We wonder if she enjoys
The enchanting hymns
Devotees sing while they sit
By her side with music and flowers

People die
We cremate them on the Hindu pyres
And float the residues in the river
Ganga absorbs all of them
As they settle into the soil
Beneath her water

Ganga has her stories to tell
Wish she had someone to listen to her
Story of her nursing the fetus
Contained in an inflated uterus
While patiently awaiting her tour
Accompanying the new life

[*Ganga* refers to the river Ganges that is commonly worshiped
by the Hindus across the globe.]

Yours Eternally

You might name it: self-questioning

Editors warn me
Obvious facts are best avoided
In poetry
But, do they consider time?

During my induction to diamond grading
The instructor lectured on four C-s

Cut
Carat
Color
Clarity

Over the years gemologists have missed out on
Another reality
Civilization!

Inside its core
A mother gives birth to light

Light links the mother
With her new family

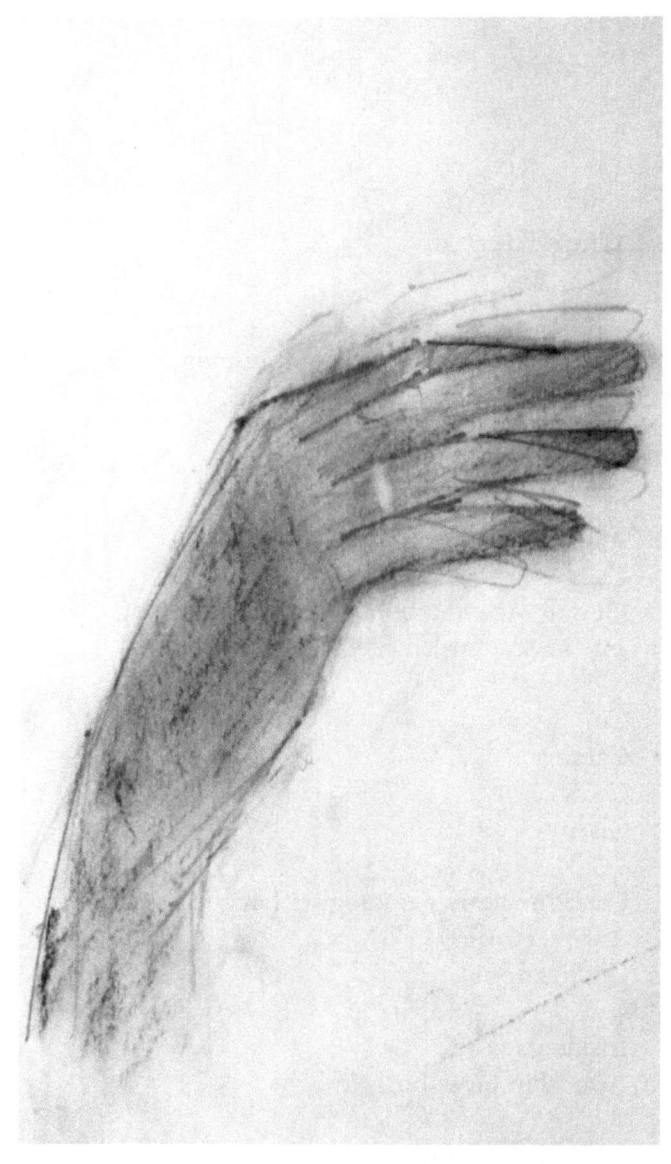

Reservation

I'm not wearing my engagement ring for years
Don't think otherwise,
I enjoy a happy married life
But then, very few of us
Take care of our fingers

It is only an occasional tingling sensation
That makes me look at my finger
I can remember the vault that has secured the ring
Since I put it off my flesh and skin!

Wish marriages came with their safety lockers

(Un)Timely Grant

The air smells heavy
Father calls up his son
He wants to offer him
The chair

Mom says, "It is too early for him,
Let my son keep afloat!"

Father is yet to inform family,
Boss has approved his prayer
and he is allowed to leave.

Struggle For Silence

Someone inquired if I was aware of existential silence

But then, how do people perceive quietude?
Is it a state of complete absence of noise?
Does clamor invite peace, by any chance?

We are, perhaps, struggling to achieve a stage
Where the flute won't sound anymore;
We will remain breathless, but relaxed
And in complete harmony with the creator!

Quiet grandeur prevails over
The pinnacle of worldly communion

www.ingramcontent.com/pod-product-compliance
Lightning Source LLC
Chambersburg PA
CBHW030518130626
46549CB00007B/3047

* 9 7 8 9 3 8 7 8 8 3 0 7 9 *